LITTLE AMBELLA

and the

LOST VALLEY

MARTIN OPIE

Little Ambella and the Lost Valley

Martin Opie

Edited and Published by
Paul Wakeling
Curlew Publications,
Tintagel, Clijah Close,
Redruth, Cornwall. TR15 2NS

Printed by Mike Williams Publicity & Promotion
Perrowford, Trefusis Road,
Redruth, Cornwall. TR15 2JN
from the publisher's typesetting

Deposited with The British Library
ISBN 0-9538456-0-5

Front cover photo :- Alison Penaluna
Back cover photo :- Sheila Griswood

Contents

Chapter		Page
	Foreword	5
	Author's Introductory Note	6
1	Little Ambella	7
2	Farming and Granite	13
3	Childhood Pastimes	19
4	Life in the Valley	26
5	Memorable Moments	31
6	The Village and its People	39
7	The End in Sight	45
8	A New Valley	49
	Outline Map of the Area	52

Foreword:

Through early recollections, Martin Opie has brought to life a taste of bygone days in rural Cornwall during and after the second World War. In this book, Martin has captured moments unique to the spirit of his childhood spent close to Stithians village.

A brief moment in time depicting simple pleasures, this is a frank, honest and charming personal account of his early life in a small pocket of West Cornwall during the 1940's and 50's, forming an interesting local historical biography. In providing us with a glimpse, Martin has added to other authors who have each given their own accounts and to those who may have shared similar times, this will doubtless rekindle further memories with equal sentiment.

Paul Wakeling.   **Autumn 1999**
Redruth, Cornwall

Author's Introductory Note

From my personal experiences I have tried to portray life in a part of rural Cornwall more than half a century ago; a glimpse of life for people who were fortunate enough to live in and around the valley of Stithians and my home at 'LITTLE AMBELLA' prior to the construction of Stithians Dam. A period that has long since disappeared, but one that enriched the lives of a few from the area, leaving us with many fond memories to reflect upon.

I wish to extend special thanks to the editor for his considerable help with this book.

Martin Opie

For my sister Esme Joyce who shared so many happy days with me at Little Ambella.

Chapter 1   *Little Ambella*

Little Ambella most certainly lies close to the dam wall itself. It was a typical Cornish smallholding comprising a cottage with outbuildings, surrounded by some 14 acres of land set in what was a beautiful valley on the outskirts of the village of Stithians in West Cornwall.

While walking across the dam wall, modern day visitors to Stithians reservoir which opened officially in 1967, will know very little of the 'Ghost' of Little Ambella and its valley which was flattened to make way for the new construction. Today, it is visited by many holiday makers and sports enthusiasts alike.

My earliest memories of Little Ambella are taken from the time when my parents moved in as tenants of this smallholding on Michaelmas day 1943, along with my 11 year old sister Esme Joyce who was almost seven years older than me.

My childhood was about to be spent in what I consider were memorable years. It was the fourth year of World War 2 and we were still in the days of blackouts even in such a remote valley as this. In the adjoining cottage lived the owner, Mrs Branch, our much loved landlady who sadly died in 1948. This left us completely without close neighbours for our remaining years there.

Inside the cottage, all cooking and boiling of water was carried out on a 'Cornish Range' stove, looking resplendent in black with brass handles and attachments.

My mother had a regular and laborious task of polishing the many brasses while cleaning the stove with a substance known as 'Black Lead'. The front room, affectionately known as the parlour, was very homely with its open fireplace.

Upstairs there were two bedrooms, though my sister preferred the parlour to sleep in. I suppose today this would be considered overcrowding. For entertainment, there was a gramophone which had to be wound up before playing one of our many scratched records. Because needles were in short supply for this type of player, each time we used it, a record was scratched that little bit more. Our sole source of contact with the outside world was by radio, powered by an accumulator which had to be charged on a regular basis at the village garage two miles away. Without this luxury, we had no news of daily events either near or far.

Lighting was provided by candles and oil lamps with a lantern to attend to the livestock on dark lonely nights. Once a week, a big galvanised bath was placed in the living room in front of the Cornish Range with water heated in saucepans to supply the family with the ritual of a weekly bath. Every bath night I remember being told not to splash water over the side; was this because someone had to follow me into the bath ? or because mother wanted to keep the floor dry ? I expect it was

A Penaluna

Looking towards Little Ambella
Our door on the left, Mrs Branch, our Landlady, on the right

R. J. Roskruge

A typical footpath on my daily trek to school

A Cornish Range -
just like the one we had at Little Ambella

a bit of both!

The toilet was a bucket inside a wooden shed in the garden where the contents had to be buried when full. Lime was always used in this, the only toilet and when visited at night, a lantern had to be carried to this outside lavatory which seemed to be the breeding quarters for huge black spiders and how primitive it all seems now.

My mother washed all large sheets in a nearby river which flowed past the entrance gate to the smallholding. She used a block of green soap, rubbing so hard that her hands had permanent blisters.The sight of those pure white sheets flapping in the breeze on the outside washing line erected in the orchard, is something that always gave me the feeling of home as a child at Little Ambella.

On the side of the house, an extension had been added for use as a dairy where all the milk was strained into churns. The dairy always felt ice - cold and was kept spotlessly clean after being scrubbed 365 days a year. The outbuildings stood on the side of the property comprising in terrace form, a feed store where rats could often be found, a cow shed partly used for rearing calves where 8 cows could be tied; next the pig sty and finally, the chicken house. At the rear of these buildings was a stable for our pony with a trap kept in an adjoining galvanised shed.

Little Ambella nestling deep in the valley, surrounded by nature with not even a glimpse of another building in sight, was tranquillity itself. Contact with neighbours required a journey of half a mile by road - a narrow rugged lane - or by public footpath across the fields. But this journey was seldom undertaken by my family who plodded on doing their own things in their own way, day in and day out.

Life could not have been easy for my parents with my father having to keep two jobs just to make ends meet. Nevertheless, they were good times and food was never in short supply.

At the front of Little Ambella were two walled gardens. On the right was an orchard and to the left was the family garden, a really pleasant country garden which extended to the river bank. The hedge by the river was a glorious sight in summer covered with wild honeysuckle, the scent of which filled the air on beautiful summer evenings. My sister had her own flower garden with cottage roses covering the arch above the entrance gate.

My father used the lower part of the garden to grow our home supply of vegetables. It was sheer bliss to wander into that garden and if father grew 30 cabbages, he could always be sure of cutting all 30 because in all the years we spent in the valley, there was never anything stolen nor did anything go missing. However, it was a different story with foxes - to which I will refer later.

Thus, the picture of life in the valley 56 years ago has been painted and I feel sure that if my parents were to return to see the modern reservoir, they would think they were on another planet. But that's not to be, both have long since passed on including my beloved sister who died at the early age of 30. Esme Joyce was born in 1931, married into the Trerise family and had a son Ian who today lives nearby. Esme passed away in 1962 and is interred in Stithians cemetery.

As for me, I have been lucky to experience life with both the old and new surroundings.

Chapter Two: *Farming and Granite*

My father was a stone mason by trade and when he took over the tenancy of Little Ambella, he knew with only 14 acres of land he could not become a full time farmer overnight. So, by combining the two a living could just about be made possible.

My mother's parents had left her enough money to purchase livestock needed for the smallholding which comprised the following: 6 cows, 4 calves, 1 sow, 5 piglets, 12 hens, and one cockerel. The pony and trap which we also kept, arrived with us. Two more cows were purchased at a later date and one of these late arrivals stands out in my memory. It was a Guernsey cow named 'Primrose' which my father bought at a farm sale near St. Day.

The distance between St. Day and our dwelling was at least six miles and both my parents undertook to walk Primrose all the way from the sale to Little Ambella. My sister and I were at home sitting on the garden wall looking up the lane eagerly awaiting their return for what seemed like an eternity until at last, all three came into view. The arrival of Primrose finally completed our stock.

I could not have imagined that decades later I would be watching a television series called 'The Good Life', which was to bring back so many happy memories. From horse carts to motors, accumulators to television and the computer age to space travel, highlights major changes that have taken place in such a short period of time.

The animals appeared to be content in their new surroundings, but disaster soon struck. We loved to see chicken running free in our orchard but hadn't taken into account 'nature' so close at hand. On one single day two foxes appeared in the orchard whereupon we witnessed them both running off carrying a chicken apiece. The following day another chicken disappeared, so we knew something had to be done before every chicken was lost to the predator. The remaining nine hens and cockerel were kept in their house for several days until a strong wire netting pen was constructed to ensure safety from the cunning fox.

.I learned to hand - milk at an early age but have to admit that when sitting on a three legged stool, receiving a swish across the face from the cow's tail in constant rhythm with the job in hand, it made me realise this was something I disliked. My father could not have appreciated me being so much smaller than him in a direct line of fire from the cow's tail, as he always felt a little annoyed. His reaction was simply to say, "get on with your job."

Each morning, father loaded the milk churns onto a hand cart then pushed it fully laden along a rugged lane to a collection point, repeating this every day in all winds and weathers before starting his second job as a stone mason.

The routine of running a smallholding seldom changed apart from haymaking time when occasionally the odd field might be ploughed. There were six fields with Little Ambella, of which two were set aside each year for the hay harvest; the process far removed from modern haymaking practice. In those days the hay was cut and hand - turned by my parents with a two pronged long - handled fork. When dry, it was stacked into piles called 'pooks' which were then collected loose by horse and wagon which had to be hired for the occasion. A hayrick was built close to the stable and I mention this because of the performance that followed. This was thatching the hayrick with rushes.

Certain parts of the valley held 'wet'rushes which grew in abundance and haymaking was never completed until the rick was thatched. My father used to purchase rushes in bundles from a man who cut and sold them to local farmers. Any straw that might be required also had to be bought, but I can remember common ferns used in place of straw.

Manure spreading was yet another task that had to be completed by hand and for this we used an 'eval', a long handled fork with five prongs. This was very hard work for a young boy but I felt sure the field I spread singlehanded, grew our best grass - though I expect my parents would have disagreed with me.

I always preferred the spring and summer months of the year and with this in mind, can recall one springtime when my father decided to plough land on the top croft which made up a part of the 14 acre smallholding. He had hoped to add another field but it proved an expensive venture to attempt to plough the croft because of all the granite stone concealed below the surface.

It never proved successful and I well remember him telling my mother, "that's the thirteenth broken ploughshare and I've only just scratched the surface." The strange thing was that throughout following summers, mushrooms always appeared in abundance over the previously ploughed ground.

It was on this top croft that I found my first and only intact skylark's nest, complete with eggs. Thankfully, the eggs all hatched despite the nest's vulnerable position so close to a pathway taken by our cattle.

The job of a stonemason was hard enough in itself without running a smallholding as well. My father had an open shed outside the entrance gate to allow for the loading of granite and it was near here that all his stonecutting work took

R. J. Roskruge

Rushes still grow in wet areas of the valley.
These were used to thatch the hayrick.

Malcolm Opie

The idyllic Tretheague Mill in Mill Lane
where our milk was collected

Cyril May

Mary May checks the pump at Carncrees, Stithians

photo - Editor

Woodlands around Stithians

place. Granite was cut mainly to order, many of which came from far outside Cornwall. The finished works were completed on a sub - contract basis for larger firms, proving a blessing for my father working on his own. He was dependent upon help in loading the heavy headstones, granite kerbstones and flowerpots which stand today in churchyards near and far - a tribute to those craftsmen of bygone days. The Cornish Stonemason certainly knew the meaning of hard work but how my father could run a smallholding as well, beats me!

Chapter Three: Childhood Pastimes

For the first three years of my childhood, I spent most of my days without playmates with the exception of my sister Esme. Despite this, I cannot recall ever feeling bored even though I spent so much time on my own. Rivers and streams gave me plenty of opportunity for fishing where medium sized trout proliferated.

My fishing experience was without rod and line, using instead a small wire meshed net with attached handle and a long stick to prod the banks to expose any fish. Several streams ran from the river to a depth just below the tops of my Wellington boots and I vividly remember endless happy hours fishing in the company of my pet cat 'Kitty Puss' - the sort of name a child might choose - she was black and white and always appreciated the odd trout or two for a riverbank feast!

Another childhood pastime was spent catching butterflies which were in abundance around the fields and hedgerows throughout the valley. No sign of modern sprays of pesticides in those days and the wild countryside lent itself to a preponderance of different species. King George, Red Admiral and Cabbage White, were among those that spring to mind. The butterflies I would collect and keep stored in jam jars in the house overnight until the next morning, whereupon my mother would make certain I released them all.

I loved to collect freshly laid hen's eggs and to encourage them further, a cloam (dummy) egg was used, enabling us to tell which hens were broody. After collecting the day's eggs, brood hens would stay in their nest boxes ruffling their feathers while making deep clucking noises. We then let the brood hens sit on 'a bakers dozen' in a galvanised housing behind a shutter for darkness and it was a great thrill when the eggs hatched allowing the chicks to follow their mothers around. Chicks hatching during May were considered weaker, so that month was avoided if possible. For fun, I often exchanged my sister's breakfast egg with a cloam one, causing much hilarity when Esme tried to break the shell!

My first recollection of Christmas at Little Ambella was in 1943 when I was thankful that Father Christmas found our home. That year left me with one wooden parrot made at Falmouth docks by a family member. It was on a pivot with a small lead weight attached to its tail allowing it to swing freely when held forward by hand. Its colour was dark green and red - what a fantastic Christmas present for a little boy ! Together with this parrot I was given one orange plus an apple with a few nuts and I considered myself lucky to have been given these presents, making my Christmas a happy one.

As with most boys I had a liking for football but in 1946 it was hard to obtain a real leather ball. My father often had a pig slaughtered for home use and this supplied me with my first ball taking the form of an inflated pig's bladder tied at the top with string, I suppose in much the same way as the very first rugby ball used on the playing fields of Rugby School early in the 19th century.

Two pitchforks were taken from the farm equipment and used to make a goal mouth. We would take turns shooting against each other and after three goals, we swapped around. It was known as 'three goals and in.' All would be fine until the pig's bladder landed with a stray kick in some bracken causing it to puncture. It was then a case of 'bracken thorn and out !' and we then had to wait for another pig to be slaughtered.

Around 1948, a school friend was given a full size genuine leather football; his father owning a piece of land suitable to play on. We each set about selecting a team, my friend's from the west of Stithians called Cascadden and my own from the north which I named Carn Rocks. The match took place at Trewithen Moor using four hay forks as goal posts. My team played with white shirts while the opposition wore mixed colours and in no time at all, the white shirts became chocolate coloured because the field had been ploughed and simply rolled level.

Several of the opposition wore steel toe-capped boots which ruined my friend's ball with scar marks, so the result was a win for the team wearing the toe-caps with the build up to the game proving more exciting than the game itself. A return fixture was avoided !

As a young boy, I had an iron hoop with driving stick and spent many an hour playing with the hoop on my own in the lanes around Little Ambella, when in 1945 families were much more relaxed about their children roaming freely in an era when national and world news was far less dramatic.

I was a small child, light enough to ride on a seat at the back of my sister's bicycle. We would travel like this to school, walking up hills and freewheeling down. My sister walked more than she cycled, but if nothing else, the bicycle was very good company for both of us.

When Esme left Stithians school at the age of 14, it was a very sad day for me. We were very close. My sister became an apprentice hairdresser with a Mrs Hambly who kept a shop above Bartles pork shop in Higher Fore Street, Redruth.

Until I was eight years old, my father took me to school but later I walked along the lane to Carn Farm down to the entrance to Carncress. From here I walked along a public footpath which crossed three fields, meeting up with another farm lane which passed the yard of Hendra Farm belonging to Mr and Mrs Richards. Once past Hendra Farm, I would walk along Hendra Road passing Stithians Church and on to school. My return journey followed the same route. There was no prospect of being driven to school or even catching a bus, unlike the luxury enjoyed by most of today's children.

Playtimes saw the craze for marbles which we collected from the tops of pop bottles where clear glass marbles were used to seal them. We purchased pop from the village shop and after drinking the contents, had a glass marble to play with.

Conkers from the horse chestnut tree were eagerly awaited every year and everyone had their own ideas about hardening them in order to win. Most boys soaked their conkers in vinegar and when a conker won one fight it was claimed to be a 'One Kinger', after three wins, a 'Three Kinger' and so on. The best I knew of was a '14 Kinger' owned by the late Hugh Carlyon. Eventually, it fought one fight too many and upon landing in the playground a cry was heard, 'Poor Hugh.'

On several days our dog Chum followed me to school. He was a large dog, an Airedale crossed with a hound. Chum used to sit patiently in the playground waiting for me to appear, ignoring older boys' attempts to tie an empty syrup tin around his neck. The boys expected him to run wild with fear but instead, he sat still holding out a paw refusing to budge, much to their annoyance. The Seven Stars public house was situated opposite the school - as it is today - and on observing the commotion, the publican would take Chum into care until father collected him when calling into the village for paraffin oil for our night lamps.

On my school route the sight of grey coloured windmills could be seen in daily use pumping water. Now, at the close of a century and with the dawning of a new era, only one or two remain in evidence, yet the introduction of windfarms generating electricity must surely be a worthwhile move. From Tretheague Mill through Stithians valley to Ponsanooth and beyond, scores of water wheels powered small industries, where today only remnants remain in evidence. Blacksmiths are a thing of the past though I can remember one at Hendra to which my father would take the pony for reshoeing. At the same time he would also take along his chisels for sharpening.

With the conclusion of the War, everyone was keen to look forward to happier times and one of those was a regular Sunday School summer outing to Carbis Bay beach. Memory of my first coach ride is uppermost in my mind when an orange and black coach aptly named 'The Marigold' took a party of us from our chapel. In 1946, the journey to Carbis Bay seemed to take forever and although only about a thirtyfive mile round trip, with slow country roads and a rickety old coach, I suppose to a young country lad it was a bit like going to the end of the earth!

My Methodist religious upbringing ensured that Esme and I regularly attended Chapel at least three times every Sunday - weather permitting. Services took place in the morning and evening with Sunday school in the afternoon. At the age of five, mother handmade my first anniversary suit with all the pins and fittings which went with it. The suit was made of red satin and I had a matching bow tie. I took to the stage of the now closed Hendra Chapel to recite my very first poem which I recall as follows:

Forget Me Not

When to the flowers so beautiful
The Father gave a name
Back came a little blue eyed one
All timidly it came
And standing by its Father's side
And gazing in his face
It said with low and trembling tones
Dear Lord the name thou gave'st me
alas I have forgot
Kindly the Father look-ed down
and said - forget me not.

I was a nervous 5 year old but remember feeling proud that the recital was well received by the Chapel congregation.

Chapter Four: *Life in the Valley*

There was one weekly caller to our home, a fish merchant called Mr. James who travelled from Porthleven with his white horse pulling a trap. All his fish were sold from open wooden boxes with nothing covered, yet it always appeared fresh. Despite open selling, we never had any poor fish and never became ill from eating any of it. Contrast this with modern times when we hear of all sorts of problems with food.

The scent of wildlife enveloped the valley around Little Ambella where we often saw badgers, foxes and rabbits. Some were almost tame and glow worms were ever present if one ventured out at night. The aroma of various wild flower and plant species ensured birds were plentiful with their calls seemingly echoing constantly about us. The memory of sweet smelling rural life and of listening to the sound of two cuckoos calling simultaneously at both ends of the valley, is something that will always remain with me.

Times were generally hard and to subsidise our diet, my father would bring home a rabbit for my mother to skin and prepare for a weekend pie.

Around nearby wet areas, frogs were plentiful enabling one or two locals to catch and sell them for around three pence each to a man known as 'froggy Moyle'. He made his profit by selling them for research direct from his storage tanks. Moles were also caught with traps and sold for a similar amount. Often throughout the summer, we blocked off a selected section of river to make a swimming pool and after completion, my mother and sister would come along so we could all have a swim together, or perhaps only a deep paddle. This was followed by a picnic on the river bank, adding up to a simple yet enjoyable day out.

On occasions, we were visited by the Home Guard who practised their shooting on a range across the valley. They seemed to spend more time at Little Ambella talking to my parents than they ever did at shooting practice. I recall one member of the Home Guard asking to use our toilet. Unfortunately, before he came on duty his sister had sewn new buttons onto his trousers to keep his braces up. Somehow she had put them in the wrong place and it wasn't until he needed to use the toilet that he realised he was wearing his trousers back to front. I doubt if he ever lived this down, judging by the laughter from his mates echoing across the valley. People saw the funny side of life in those days and I cannot recall ever hearing the word 'stress' crop up in conversation as it does so readily today.

During 1943/44, evacuees from London came to stay with families in the area. Several children lived with families in Stithians. Father went along to the village hall with instructions from mother to accept one girl around the same age as my sister. It was felt this would help to settle her in and would make good company for Esme. At the selection evening there were two sisters whom father considered shouldn't be separated, so he brought both girls home with him. They had to share a bed with my sister making three in a bed ! The sisters were from Bromley in Kent and their names were Joan and Nyria Simpson. Their brother Peter stayed with another local family.

On one occasion following heavy rainfall, Joan waded into the river up to her waist to save several tiny ducklings. After great effort, the ducklings were safe but Joan struggled back to the shore. My father had only recently bought them and was very grateful to her, but would gladly have forgone their recovery knowing how tricky the waters were with such a depth.

I often wonder if the two girls ever reflect upon their stay at Little Ambella during wartime, or even if they are aware of its change with new valley and reservoir. In my early 20's, I visited Nyria in London prior to her marriage. Joan studied medicine and became a Doctor but unfortunately, contact with the family has been lost over the years.

Another three years elapsed before a family of eight came to live a quarter of a mile away at Carnvullock Cottage. They were the Hughes family with 6 children and their names were, Ted, Pat, Jessica, Roger, Angela and Trevor. I was the same age as the second child Pat, but the whole family were a godsend and my sister and I really hit it off with all of them. What a difference this made to my life in 1946.

Unknown to me until relatively recently, Angela Hughes eventually had a daughter and named her after my sister Esme. Also, Pat and Jessica have visited Esme Joyce's grave twice a year to place flowers and this was another revelation to me and a rather uplifting thought. Certainly a measure of the closeness of our two families.

Every year, my father hired a black and green car from a local undertaker, a Mr. William J. Martin, which enabled both the Hughes and our family to spend a day at the seaside at Portreath. We were each allowed one ice-cream, holding on to its taste throughout the rest of the year!

On one memorable occasion, one of father's cows was ready to give birth to a calf at any time, so he couldn't take us all the way but dropped us off at Redruth, whereupon we all caught a bus called 'The Silver Queen'. This ran a return journey to Portreath from Downing's barber shop in Penryn Street. The process of getting to the beach was almost as exciting as actually setting foot on the sand. Happy carefree days; the simple things in life with none of us given too much luxury to spoil us. Would it satisfy today's children I wonder?

With the advent of the Hughes family taking up residence, birthday parties were much more fun. The month of August couldn't come soon enough for me with many outdoor games like hide and seek followed by a massive birthday tea with Mrs Hughes coming along to give my mother a helping hand.

In the winter of 1947 I remember my remote home for many different reasons: Its heavy snowfall, which saw us isolated for several days; no school; no collection of farm milk; no visitors and towards the end of the week because we were unable to get the accumulator charged - no radio! Snow reached as high as the field hedgetops to a depth which meant I couldn't go outside, so the record player was used continuously.

My mother seemed to spend a whole week with pans of milk forever on the Cornish Range making cream and butter from all our unsold milk and I am sure because of the quantity of cream produced, I have been put off eating any for over half a century!

After the snow had cleared, my mother took me to the neighbouring hamlet of 'Shop Pool' which today is known as Goonlaze. The shop was just a small wooden building with a lady owner who sold many items. On collecting my sweets she remarked to my mother that I "knew like human." Coming out of the shop my mother was most upset and remarked to me, "that silly old woman saying you know like human - you *are* human!" My mother seemed unusually bothered by the remark, but now, much later in life as I pass through Goonlaze, there is no sign of the shop or keeper.

Life at Little Ambella and surrounding valley could, at times, feel very lonely in winter and I always held the feeling that mother never liked being left alone at the cottage with two children when my father went into the village on the odd winter's evening. Upon his return she would often ask him, "have you seen anyone on your journey home ?" His reply was invariably, "I haven't come into contact with anyone worse than myself!" However, on one occasion he returned home rather shaken when a badger crossed the lane in front of his bicycle sending him over the handlebars. He was lucky it happened nearby as he limped home to tell the tale.

Brought up in the country, I respected the countryside and have always had a soft spot for wildlife such as badgers and foxes. Even as a young boy, unknown to my parents, I left scraps of food at an entrance to a foxes den because I felt sorry for them out in the wild on cold nights.

I was a country boy in every sense of the word and my heart was forever warmed at the thought of growing up around Little Ambella. It was the simple but natural things in life which allowed me no time to feel bored. What happy and carefree childhood days they were.

Chapter Five: *Memorable Moments*

As mentioned, the radio was a constant source of information and amusement. One night, while listening to coverage of a boxing match between Bruce Woodcock and Joe Baski, the entire family was gathered around the set. As the fight intensified, great excitement developed and after listening to several rounds our accumulator went flat. To this day I couldn't tell you who won the contest yet it brings a smile to my face when I think of the power to our radio gradually fading with everyone huddled around listening.

On another dark winter's night shortly after 1945, we were all sitting around the kitchen table with drawn back curtains and an oil lamp burning when a face appeared close to the glass window pane. A tramp stood holding up his can for fresh drinking water, so father went outside to see what the man wanted, with my mother closing the door behind him. Locking father outside with the stranger, no harm came from that poor old traveller who was well off the beaten track in the remote valley. After replenishment the tramp went on his way again.

Our drinking water came from a very deep well in the first field next to the property. To fill a bucket, it was fixed to a chain which was lowered then wound up again. The well was open at the top and would certainly not be allowed today.

In about 1946, my father made me a nice strong catapult. One day I spied our big white cockerel standing on the top stone surrounds of the well. He'd escaped from his pen and was crowing his head off. I picked up my catapult, took aim some yards away and with a small stone, hit the bird clean off the ledge with my first shot, only to see it disappear flapping down the well into our source of drinking water. It took my father two days to retrieve the drowned cockerel and from then on, all our water had to be boiled. How I learned my lesson for this action; as a result, the first hard smack I can recall with no radio, no record player and early to bed for a whole week !

The valley was renowned for its adders. The snakes were quite long and their skin pattern resembled that of a mackerel with 'V' markings. They are quite venomous creatures and before the reservoir was built, they were plentiful around Little Ambella and Carn Rocks. I often wonder where they have all gone and if they are still breeding. In those days you would never miss one on a bright sunny summer's day.

On one particular day, I spotted an adder resting on top of a granite stone elevated above the ground; the stones colloquially known as 'grass rocks'. The adder had her young all around her and on spying me, swallowed them up for safety. After all was clear, she regurgitated them when peace returned once more to the valley.

There were times when life seemed cruel and some events would these days seem bizarre. This brings me to one of the most memorable incidents that happened involving one of those infamous snakes.

It was a late summer's evening and my mother remained downstairs reading a book with light provided by an oil lamp after the rest of the family had turned in for the night. As usual, mother let our dog outside for ten minutes before closing up and herself retiring to bed. That ten minutes brought about an extraordinary event.

Unknown to anyone, an adder had entered our house through the open door on that balmy summer night. Every morning, before my father carried out the milking, his first job would be to light the fire in the Cornish Range. This enabled the family to start another day with a pot of tea. After cleaning the fire ashes and laying new sticks, he would check the oven for any baking tins which may have been left inside from the previous day. On looking inside the oven, he was confronted with a 'Hiss'. I can hear his voice as if it were only yesterday yelling, "There's an adder in the oven !" I ran downstairs with my mother who asked my father what he intended doing about it. His reply was simply, "I have no alternative but to roast it alive otherwise I will be bitten by it." The snake must have crept past my mother's feet while she was reading her book the previous evening.

During the night, the adder presumably headed for the warmest part of the house entering the oven through its open door to settle in comfort. The fire was charged up to the full as we sat quaking, listening to the thumping of that poor adder inside the increasingly hot oven. After about an hour, when all was still, father opened the oven door and there for all to see was the shrivelled up cooked adder which was duly removed using a hand brush and fire shovel.

Mother was certainly lucky not to have been bitten that night as she quietly read her book while waiting quietly for Chum to return to the house. No thought of asking for help from anyone; no-one available and no RSPCA assistance like today.

R. J. Roskruge

Mill Lane, today largely unspoilt,
where my father pushed the handcart with milk churns

Typical stream of the area, feeding today's reservoir

One winter's night, I became very upset. It was about 3.00 am when we were woken by a man who lived about a mile away. He wanted to show us that he'd shot two badgers. There he stood with a lantern and shotgun with one badger over his back and another over his chest. I recall looking down from the bedroom window with my mother who was also upset as she said to him, 'You're a cruel man and want locking up!' There are few sad memories from the valley, but this was certainly one of them.

Fifty-five years ago, motor bikes with sidecars were in abundance around the roads and my parents often recalled one particular occasion involving a combination.

Before they were married, my father had a motorcycle on the back of which my mother refused to ride. Mother had a job in the Post Office and general stores at Fraddon, north of Truro. She lodged from Sunday evening until Friday whereupon father would collect her from work that evening each week.

Halfway between Tresillian and Truro there was once an infamous bend in the trees known as 'woodcock corner'. It was here that the base of my father's sidecar parted from the frame holding it to the motorbike, taking my mother with it. This all occurred with father completely oblivious to what was happening as he continued for a further half mile into Truro. He apparently blamed it on poor visibility while his goggles were down. Still, he returned to the wooden-based sidecar, collected his fiancée - as she then was - delivered her home safely and later married her.

Early days of transport took some getting used to for my mother. On one Good Friday, the family took a rare day out in the borrowed Austin motor BXY 264. We decided to go cockling or, (picking 'Trig') at the Helford. Just before the descent to Helford Passage lies a steep hill which my mother refused to negotiate whilst sitting in the car. She got out and walked the short distance to the shore leaving my father, sister and me to trust the car's brakes to take us down the hill. Many times we laughed about it though no-one could persuade mother to remain in the car at that particular spot.

One weekend my father brought home from the village a pair of young homing pigeons which he thought would make a good distraction for me from other pursuits. He introduced me to a red hen with a blue cock bird and I was thrilled to have my very own pets. A tea chest on the wall just inside the orchard was to provide their accommodation. I kept them inside the tea chest for several weeks before letting them out to fly.

All went well for the first week when they flew around returning home to their nest, but early in the second week of flight, the red hen developed a habit of perching on the chimney. Towards the end of that week it went missing and we simply could not find it, as far as we were concerned the hen was lost.

On the second night of its disappearance my sister heard

something moving inside the parlour chimney breast. Whatever was there, it was alive ! The next day, father got out the flu brush to sweep the chimney. "It's that pigeon!" he exclaimed. "I'm sure, stuck on a ledge just out of reach above the fireplace." In order to reach the pigeon, father had to make a hole in the parlour wall and this turned out to be an extremely time consuming job. Time and again I'm sure he wished he hadn't thought of the idea of pigeons for me. One day I had a fortunate escape from serious injury. While crossing a field of nearby Carnmeor farm, a Jersey cow who had recently had her calf, charged toward me at full tilt presumably thinking I was a threat. I immediately ran towards the hedge but the cow managed to catch and pin me against it with her horns. If it hadn't been for farmer Ben Martin who happened by chance to be there, perhaps I would not have survived so I owe him a huge debt of gratitude for getting me out of a tight corner.

Chapter Six: The Village and its People

Stithians village lying two miles from Little Ambella, was the centre for entertainment during the 1940's and 50's and it seemed everyone had to walk in order to get anywhere. The day a circus came to the village was memorable for one particular local character.

For the main performance, my father booked advance tickets for the family. The big top was located in the village playing field opposite the school and although only a small circus, I was looking forward to it for days. It held a local flavour and children like me were naturally very excited by it.

During one performance the chapel organist was 'set up' by the circus ring master who put him in a selected seat. The ring master asked a pony to go towards the audience and nod its head at the biggest drinker in Stithians. Of course, the pony selected the chapel organist - who was renowned for indulging in the 'odd tipple'- whereupon everyone howled with laughter and took great delight in reminding the organist for weeks after.

Waiting for the thrill of a visit from the mobile cinema with the owner's exciting black and white western films was another of my recollections. Nowadays such events are confined to history but to youngsters of yesteryear, these films seemed the dawning of a new age.

From as far back as I can remember, several village people were known by their nick-names instead of their correct names. Three that readily spring to mind are John Dunstan, Cecil Opie and Reginald Trerise. John played the part of a cat in a school play and was readily named 'whiskers'. Cecil regularly played cards at the local public house and always seemed to hold low numbered cards commonly referred to as 'spotters'. Naturally, he was known as 'spotter'. Reginald would often swim with his friends in a nearby river and one day, around the time that Burgess swam the English Channel, he uttered a yell, "I am Burgess !" securing him of his nickname. Sadly, these characters are no longer with us.

This might seem trivial to people unused to a quiet village life, but it was late 1940's Stithians, a country backwater where everyone had to create their own fun.

Changes witnessed in my lifetime have not been confined to my home in the lost valley. During that time I have seen changes to the structure of the village itself. I remember nine shops as thriving businesses, yet today with the dominance of the car and supermarket we have only one. Although a chapel, church, public house, hotel, post office, food store, fish & chip shop, hairdresser, garage for repairs, plus a filling station with comprehensive building supplies, is sufficient for most rural dweller's needs.

The village school, which I attended with my late sister more than half a century ago, still stands proudly on the same site and long may it continue to educate local people.

The vicarage was located opposite the village church and is now The Old Vicarage Hotel. Many of the hard working locals remain in Stithians today and one such gentleman in his eighties remarked recently upon seeing a teenage couple embrace in the street, "It was never like this when I was a young man. Every sunday after church we would meet local girls for a chat and after a little while, go home." This prompted me to write the following poem in the hope that further memories might be rekindled:

Sunday Nights

The week passed by so slowly for the local village lads
When all they longed for every day was the week to come
and pass
They knew each Sunday night to be the highlight of their
week
It was when the local boys and girls conveniently would
meet
The time and place it never changed 7.30 on the dot
Around this time they knew for sure the vicar had
preached his lot
The boys stood outside the village church the girls
would then appear
About a dozen local maids all dressed in Sunday gear
The lads they too looked very smart with Brylcreme in
their hair
Their shining shoes which mothers cleaned gave them a
manly air
It added to that Sunday scene as they just waited there
To meet the girls and have a chat no trouble nor a care
They spent the week preparing 'twas all they'd waited
for
And then they went their separate ways to wait that week
once more...

The Parish Church of St Stythians

A disused, flooded quarry

Little Ambella

Stithians Dam
"Can the present visitor, walking across the dam,
feel the presence of Little Ambella?"

Local characters were the salt of the earth. One such person was Charlie Thomas of Foundry. Charlie worked at the local quarry and seemed to have a new tale to tell every other day. Like the story of a quarry worker who visited a nearby town to purchase a cap. After looking at several he turned to the shop assistant and said, "you don't seem to stock what I'm looking for." "What are you looking for sir ?" "Oh, just an ordinary cap for work - with a peak in the back !"

During the war around 1944, many American servicemen visited the village from their nearby camp. My father told us of their liking for gin which was in short supply and of a local man who discovered a way of 'making a few bob' for himself. He would collect empty gin bottles from local pubs, purchase one full bottle and pour half the gin into one empty bottle, leaving a half in the other. Both bottles were then topped up with water and resealed, giving him two full bottles to sell to the Americans who never detected the watered - down gin.

Today we hear of all sorts of crime, but I wonder how much 'bootlegging' went on like this during wartime Britain?

Chapter Seven: *The End in Sight*

One evening, father returned home after a visit to the village. He appeared ill at ease and rather sad. His discussion with my mother made my ears prick up. He said that it appeared a new reservoir was likely to be built around our home and we must prepare for our future as the end was now in sight. If it were true, we obviously had no choice, but none of us wanted to leave the valley. All continued as normal for the next three months until one morning, workmen appeared close to our home where their task was to dig trial bore holes, erecting what at first looked like small telephone boxes.

Their equipment recorded the flow of water down stream and it was at this point that I realised Little Ambella was doomed. That afternoon after school, I walked up to my favourite childhood spot at Carnvullock Bridge where most of my early fishing was done. It was such a lovely spot; the bridge rather worn through time and becoming unfit to take road transport. In fact, transport always passed in front of the bridge via a ford.

As I sat upon the bridge daydreaming, I thought to myself that no other place would mean so much to me; no other place would mean anything to me by comparison. Little Ambella was all I had known, it was and always will be, my home. I was familiar with every stepping stone which bisected the river in that valley and thought, 'Why should someone else come along to spoil it and what right do they have to claim it as theirs ?'

Several local people remarked that it would prove to be a 'white elephant' and that no reservoir would be built, yet my parents who had lived with the running water flowing past their entrance gate each day, knew differently. With this in mind, our family had to make plans to leave even before any planning decision had been made regarding the construction of the main reservoir wall.

Father had heard that someone from Devon was looking for a shorthold tenancy of a small holding and after several meetings, it was agreed that the Devonian farmer would take over the tenancy until a larger farm more suitable for his requirements became available. Before moving in, the farmer agreed to take over all our stock which was a blessing to my mother as at least the animals would be spared the Auctioneer's hammer. So, we purchased a cottage in a nearby hamlet for a brief time until returning once again to Stithians village to live.

My father gave up his two jobs as a mason and farmer to drive for a local firm of undertakers until his death some years hence.

Upon our return to Stithians, it allowed me to witness the construction of the dam and to picture the reservoir with altered valley in the knowledge that few would recall the lost valley and the 'ghost' of Little Ambella.

During August 1962, excavation began to establish the foundations of what is today Stithians Dam. By October 1962, there was a wall spanning a length of 800 feet with a height 140 feet from the foundations to its centre and by 1963, most nearby residents had vacated their homes. It was to be another five years before a commissioning ceremony was held on 13th October 1967.

Little Ambella was unique in being one of the most isolated properties which succumbed to the reservoir's surface area of 274 acres although various other farm dwellings disappeared and were subsequently lost forever. To name a few they were, Colvennor and Carnvullock; North and East Menorlue; Higher and South Ambella farms, with some two dozen private dwellings falling victim to the contractor's bulldozers working relentlessly to bring about the completion of a new valley.

My Home:

Where homes once stood there's water
Millions of gallons a day
Supplying need to towns and villages
Which meant we could not stay
Now all we have are memories
And a line in history books
But it holds a place within my heart
It was MY home that they took
A child's mind wanders freely
but memories never fade
The ghost of Little Ambella
Is one that always stays

Chapter Eight: *A New Valley*

In the new valley of today, recreation on Stithians reservoir is apparent. Before its construction, residents received visits from only a handful of people. Now there are walkers, fishermen, sailors, ornithologists, canoeists, school parties and general holiday makers. Cameras click and people picnic, a complete contrast to 55 years ago.

Peace and tranquillity is still possible if one casts an eye across the shimmering water and with such a vast area to choose from, visitors' views are plentiful though I have two favourite spots of my own. They are at 'Roger's Mount' at the Carnmenellis section of the reservoir and The Golden Lion Inn at Menherion, where the weary traveller may find substantial meals and refreshments.

A link with the past exists today if one takes the lane to the left of the car park along the new valley. It is known as Mill Lane and runs along to the collection point that my father used daily to push his handcart with milk churns to Little Mill. These days I regard Mill Lane as memory lane where the old leat can still be seen lower down on the left hand side. Water trickles along its path where once it passed more quickly to Tretheague Mill to drive the water wheel almost a century ago. The water wheel is no longer there but a short distance away, the owners of Tregonning Mill have restored their wheel superbly, to hold onto memories of bygone days.

As with similar constructions, the aim of Stithians reservoir was to supply much needed water to a vast number of people over a wide area and with a capacity to hold 1,200 million gallons with a depth in excess of 60 feet at its maximum, this it certainly has done. Yet, I cannot help wondering if residents of today would so easily have given up their homes without presenting a stronger protest. 1990's Britain, with speedier communication, is very different to that of the early 1960's when it was usually frowned upon to delay 'progress'.

I still hold mixed feelings having witnessed the old and new but my sincere hope is that the present day visitor enjoys the new valley with altered scenery.

For those who are interested, full details of the unusual arched dam construction and reservoir appear in several publications with perhaps the July 1986 A.H.S. issue, (Aspects of History in Stithians), as informed as any. This was compiled by members of Stithians local history group.

Recently, I noticed children playing around the reservoir in the same area as I had 55 years earlier and with much emotion, I wrote the following which I considered a fitting end to my story of Little Ambella and the lost valley:

Childhood Games:

A child will always play the games that little children do
And will not give a second thought to life that beckons you
It's only when much older we reflect on childhood games
And think of all that's gone before and of those younger days
Now all that's left are memories with slippers and a pipe
Because I'm getting older my childhood out of sight
At last I'm glad to have realised that what is best for me
Is leave those childhood games once played to younger
folk than me......

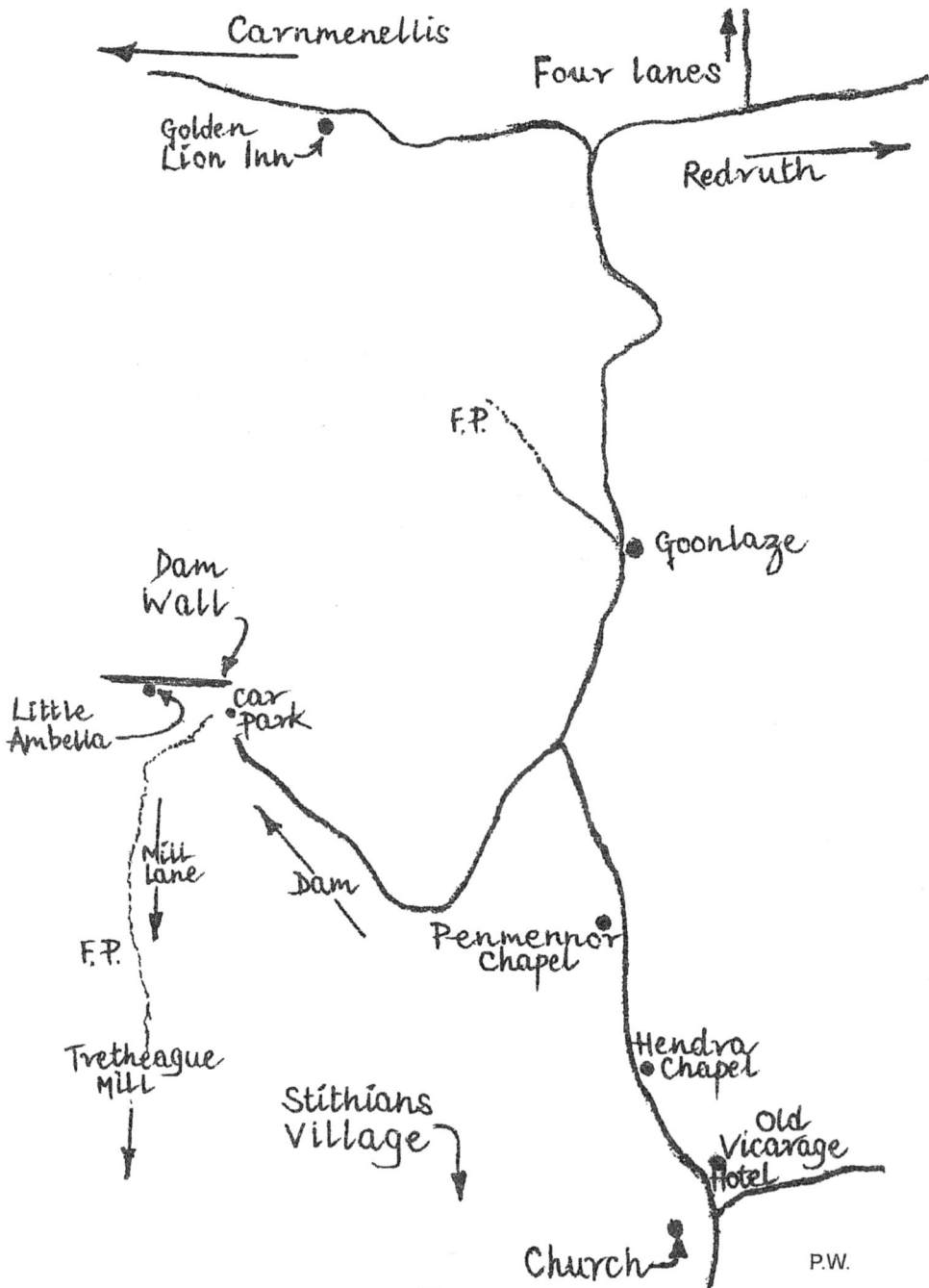

Carnmenellis

Four lanes

Golden Lion Inn

Redruth

F.P.

Goonlaze

Dam Wall

Little Ambella

Car Park

Mill Lane

Dam

Penmennor Chapel

F.P.

Hendra Chapel

Tretheague Mill

Old Vicarage Hotel

Stithians Village

Church

P.W.

52